**EARLY LEARNING**
For three- to five-year-o

# The Moonlit Cat

Story by Pie Corbett
Activities by David Bell, Pie Corbett
Geoff Leyland and Mick Seller

Illustrations by Diann Timms

For Matthew

Jenny was always losing things.

Have you ever lost anything special?

Hide something behind your back and ask your friends to guess what it is. You can give them three clues, for example, what size it is, whether you play with it, whether it has wheels.

The night that Jenny lost her lucky charm, Mum was really cross.

Why do you think Mum was so cross?

Why was the charm so special?

What is a lucky charm?

What special things do you have? As you read the story, look in the pictures for the charm.

Jenny lay asleep, dreaming.

Look closely at Jenny's dream.
Try to name all the things that you
can see in it.

How many animals can you see?
How many plants can you see?
How many metal things can you see?
How many wooden things can you see?

Baby lay asleep, dreaming.

Look at all the different-shaped boxes.

Look for shapes like this:

Look for shapes like this:

What do you think is in the different boxes?

Something woke Jenny up.
Was it the tree tapping?
Was it the gate creaking?
Was it a car hooting?
Was it the fridge grumbling?

Listen carefully to the noises you can hear around you.

What do you think they are?

What or who might be making the sound?

# No. It was something downstairs.

Jenny is tiptoeing downstairs.
Imagine that she is counting the stairs as she goes.
Can you help her count?

Ask a grown-up to cut out some cats from a folded piece of paper.
When you unfold the paper, how many cats are there joined together?

A cat white as the moon.

Jenny let her in.

She had stars in her eyes and shone like the moonlight.

Draw some full moon shapes, like this: ○

Draw some crescent moons, like this: ☾

Try to draw some patterns with these shapes.
Look out of the window before you go to bed.
Can you see the moon?

The Moonlit Cat led Jenny through the dark of the house.

They were looking for something; the cat purred.

What would you use in the dark to help you see?
Make a collection of things to shine your torch through, such as a piece of paper, a book, a handkerchief, a pillow, and a hat.
So that they don't get too warm, hold each item to the torch for a few seconds only.
Sort them into two piles: one pile of things that torchlight shines through, and one of things that torchlight does not shine through.

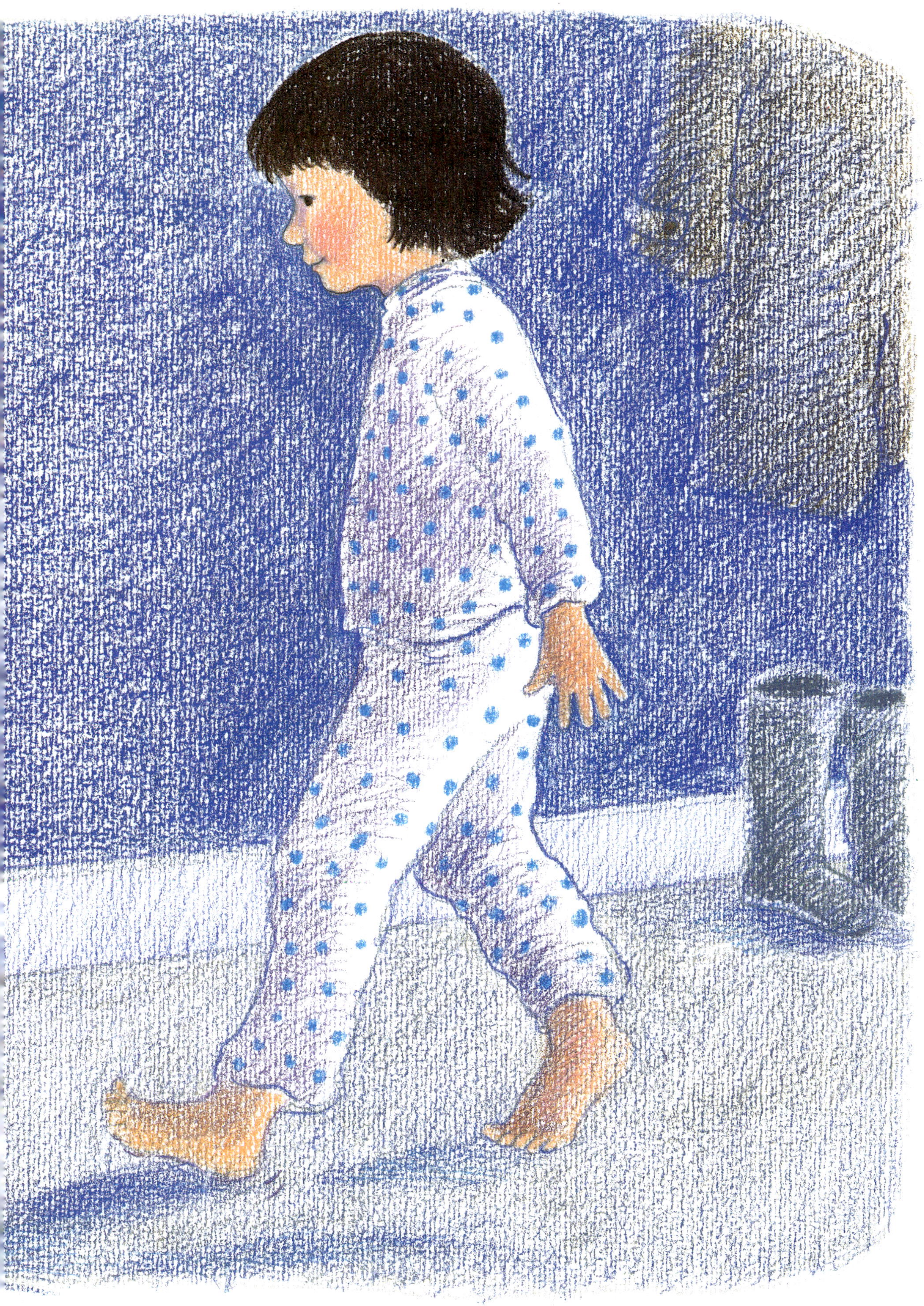

They passed through dark caves of dreams...

What can you see in the picture?
What is right in front of Jenny?
What is behind the Moonlit Cat?
Point to the quickest way Jenny and the cat can go.

...they passed through palace halls, dimly lit...

Talk about times when you can see things easily
- as in the daytime, and times when it's difficult
to see things - as in the dark.
How can you tell what things are when you can't
see them?

Play the 'touch and guess' game with someone.
Close your eyes while they put something in
your hands.
Can you guess what it is without looking?

...they climbed
snow-capped mountains...

Are the mountains real?
Is Jenny awake or asleep?

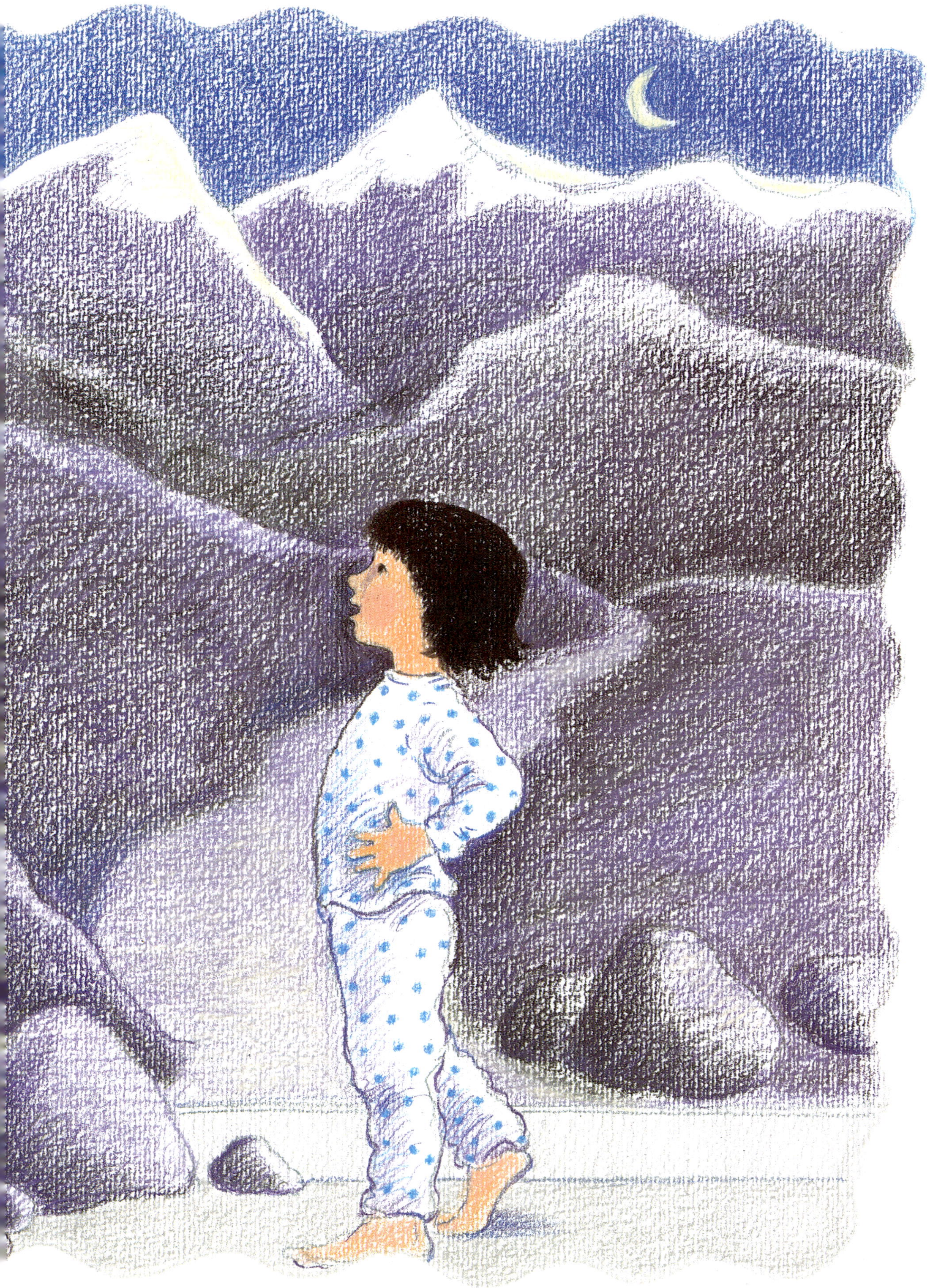

...and crossed the deserts of the night.

What do you think is going to happen?
Have you ever tiptoed in the darkness?
How do you think Jenny feels?

In Baby's dream, Jenny saw what they were looking for.

Look at the toys in the factory. How could you sort them out?

By colour? Do that.

By type of toy? Do that.

By size? Do that.

You could try getting out some of your own toys and sorting them in different ways.

Jenny and the Moonlit Cat
had found her lucky charm.

Play the 'find the treasure' game.

Choose six toys. Ask a grown-up to cut out a paper charm shape and hide it under one of the toys.

Try to guess which one it's hidden under by asking questions such as 'Is it under the biggest toy?' or 'Is it under the toy with wheels?'.

You can only ask questions where the answer is 'yes' or 'no'. When you have guessed the hiding place, it is your turn to hide the charm and answer the questions.

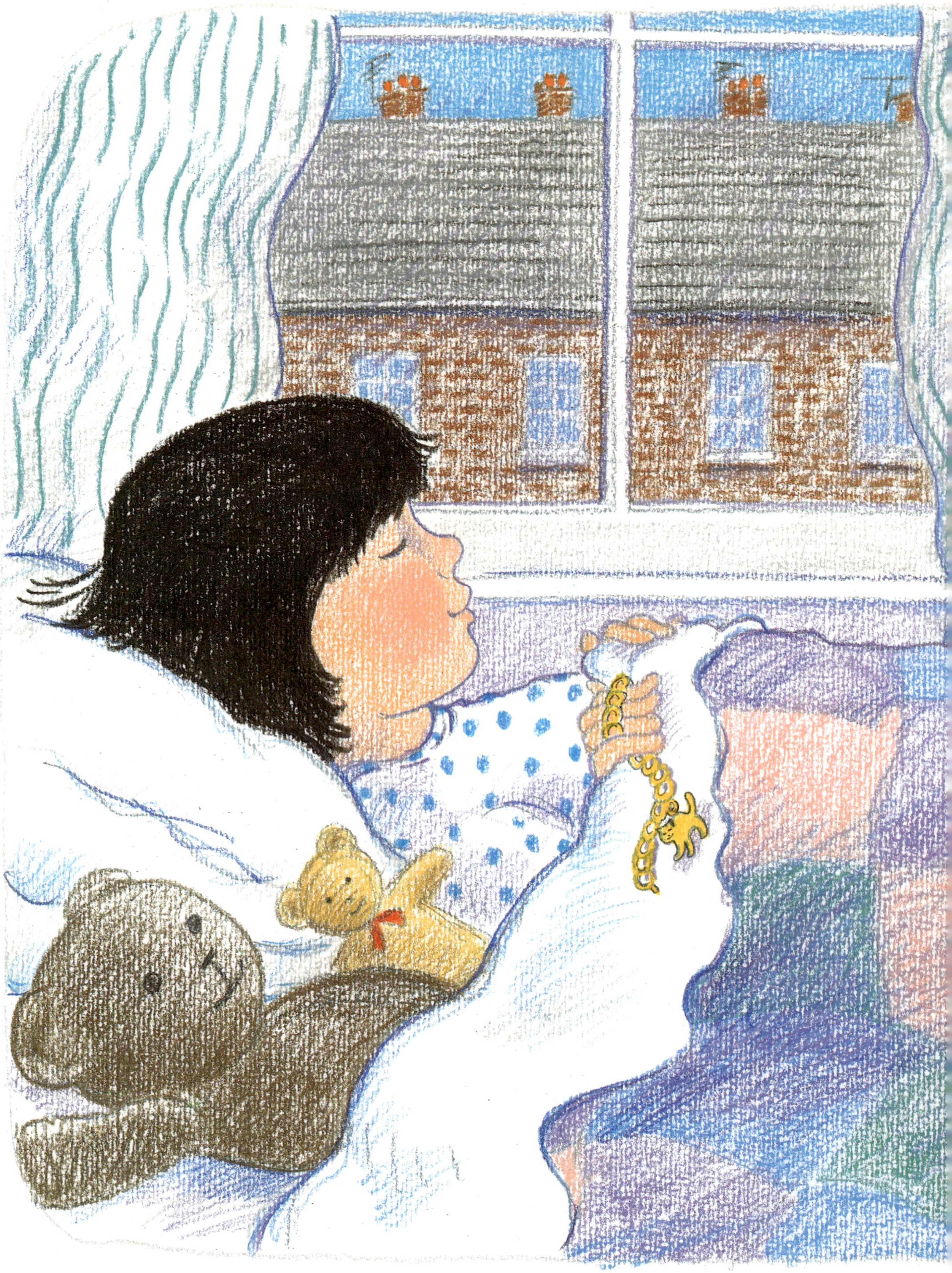

Can you remember what woke Jenny up?

What did she do next?

Where did the Moonlit Cat take Jenny in her dream?

Where did they go first?

Where did they go last?

# Activity Notes

**Pages 2-3** Children enjoy this sort of guessing and describing game - and it helps them to develop their vocabulary. Learning to live with loss is a theme of many books for young children. This story is about finding things, too. Treasure hunts such as 'Hunt the Easter Egg' or putting a tooth under a pillow are traditional activities which play an important part in growing up.

**Pages 4-5** It is important to help your child 'read' the pictures. Ask questions such as 'Can you show me the mummy?' and 'Can you see the cat?'. Build on these by interpreting the pictures with questions such as 'How does the little girl feel?'. You can also encourage your child to predict by asking 'What do you think will happen?'.

**Pages 6-7** As children count up each category, they must sort the objects into groups: animals, plants etc. This is practice for the important skill of classification. Extend the activity by collecting animal pictures and sorting them according to questions. 'Do they... live on the land or in the sea... have fur or feathers... have four, six or eight legs... lay eggs or have babies?' Gradually make your questions more difficult.

**Pages 8-9** Young children often confuse two- and three-dimensional shapes. They need experience in recognising the common three-dimensional shapes and this can be encouraged by spotting similar shapes to the ones in this book around and outside the house.

**Pages 10-11** Different objects make different associated sounds and some are more difficult to hear than others. Develop this idea by collecting together several objects that make a noise. Ask someone to make a sound with each, out of sight of the listener. Try to identify each sound in turn. Are some more difficult than others? Talk about why this is.

**Pages 12-13** Counting activities can take place every day and these help to make maths fun. Going up and down stairs is a simple activity and children can count each step as they climb up or come down.

**Pages 14-15** Most children are fascinated by the moon and stars: to them they seem magical. When they draw a C moon or an O moon, make sure that they draw the patterns going anticlockwise, as if they were letter shapes. This sort of fun with patterns helps pencil control and will make handwriting easier.

**Pages 16-17** This activity is an investigation of how some materials allow light to pass through them more easily than others. Using two torches, play 'Chase the Beam' or 'Copycat'. One person shines the beam on a wall while the other chases or copies a simple pattern.

**Pages 18-19** Children learn directional language through following simple instructions. This is best done in a matter-of-fact way as children carry out simple tasks around the house.

**Pages 20-21** Without light, many things become difficult - not just identifying objects. Draw a simple picture or pattern in the dark, then repeat it in good light. Compare the two results. What else could you try to show the difference?

**Pages 22-23** Talking about the story helps to deepen our understanding of it. It doesn't matter if your child thinks the mountains are real or not. Stories can be read and enjoyed at different levels. Perhaps the story needs to retain its air of mystery.

**Pages 24-25** One of the ways in which we read is by constantly guessing what is going to come next. If you read a story to your child a number of times, you will notice that they learn the story by heart. Try reading part of the sentence on a page and let your child finish it. Let them tell you the story. This is an early stage of learning to read and an exciting sign of your child's development.

**Pages 26-27** Children can sort out items according to set criteria such as colour or size. However, they should also be encouraged to sort out items according to their own criteria which can be discussed.

**Pages 28-29** Early scientific investigations often require children to be systematic when performing tasks and asking questions. Playing card games such as 'Pairs' will help them to develop this skill and will also improve their memories.

**Pages 30-31** Children have a very limited understanding of the passage of time. This can be developed by asking them to place activities in sequence during the day. Use language such as 'firstly', 'secondly', etc.